Tightrope ...

Balancing Faith, Ministry and Cancer

Cullen Bryant Wilson

Tightrope ...

Balancing Faith, Ministry and Cancer

A Pastor's Journey Through Cancer

Editor Christy Smith
Cullen Bryant Wilson

Copyright © Cullen Bryant Wilson

All rights reserved. No part of this book may be used or reproduced by any means, graphic, electronic or mechanical, including photocopying, recording or taping or by any information storage retrieval system without the written permission of the publisher except in the case of brief quotations embodied in critical articles and reviews.

Whosoever Press books may be ordered through booksellers or by contacting:

Whosoever Press
P.O. Box 1513
Boaz, AL 35957
www.whosoeverpress.com
1-256-706-3315

Because of the dynamic nature of the Internet, any web addresses or links contained in this book may have changed since publication and may no longer valid. The views expressed in this work are solely those of the author and do not necessarily reflect the views of the publisher, and the publisher hereby disclaims any responsibility for them.

ISBN-13: 978-0-9987724-5-5

Library of Congress Control Number: Applied For

Printed in the United States of America

Whosoever Press date: 8/5/2017

Table of Contents

Foreword	1
Purpose	3
Acknowledgements	5
Discovery	6
There Is A River	8
A Healing Adventure	9
Hugs Are Better Than Drugs	11
Hitting The Wall	13
Psalm 1	15
On Choices	17
The Path	19
Who Am I?	21
God's 2x4	23
Hello, Again	25
How're You Doing?	28
I Have ALL The Answers	30
Caged Up	32
Promises! Promises!	34
The News	36
A Mop-Up Operation	38
Hang In There	40
For All The Right Reasons	42
Prayer, Healing and Miracles	44
Doing The Grown-Up Thing	46
Can I Go To Disneyland Instead?	48
The Skinhead Blues	50
I've Got Something To Say	51
In Limbo	53
Washed Out … But Not Up	55
He Lives	57
A Second Chance	59
Day By Day	61
What Now?	63
Resurrection	65
Re-Entry	67

From Scratch	69
Winners and Losers	71
Be At Rest Once More, O My Soul	73
Tug of War	75
Tightrope	77
Battleground	79
But If Not	81
Obituary Notice	83
Neutral	84
News Clips	87

Foreword

C. Bryant Wilson was a friend of mine. In fact, he was my best friend for over 30 years. Although we seldom lived in the same town, or even the same state, Bryant refused to let our friendship fade. If I went a couple of months without writing, he was on the phone wanting to know why. Very few years passed when one of us was not spending his precious vacation time visiting the other, and I will always cherish those memories and be grateful that I was fortunate to have known him as well as I did. In fact, had I not known him, I probably would not be around today. He was there for me during my darkest hours. His understanding of human nature and his ability to help me work through my feelings of insecurity and hopelessness enabled me to survive, and ultimately, thrive. Without his influence, his concern and his love, I doubt I would have made it. But these writings are not about me; they are about Bryant and the product of his own trauma.

A virulent form of cancer attacked him during the prime years of his life, and he had to undergo a long, and arduous regimen of chemotherapy, radiation, and even a bone marrow transplant. Anyone who has been through that ordeal, or has known anyone who has, understands it is not for the faint or weak of heart.

Bryant not only endured, he carefully and unselfishly wrote down his thoughts, hopes and dreams as he faced his own impending death. I suspect this was to a large extent a cathartic effort for him, but in doing so he also touched the hearts and minds of those around him. He never lost hope, in spite of the failure of the treatments to arrest the cancer, and he continued his writing right up until the end came.

Bryant Wilson would not have wanted to be remembered as something he wasn't. He was not a saint, but simply a very good man who felt it was his calling to help others. It is my hope now that his writings will live on, to be there to offer solace to others having to undergo a similar ordeal. In the 20 years or so since his untimely death at the young age of 51, treatments have improved dramatically, and there is greater hope for today's victims of the tragic ailment we lump under the rubric "cancer." It is also my hope that Bryant's writings will be there to help give them the strength, hope and vigor to endure and survive. I know that is what my friend, C. Bryant Wilson, would have wanted.

Earl W. Boatwright, Ph.d

Purpose

The times of greatest pageantry and celebration in the life of the Church, in the gathered community of faith, in the family are often times when death strikes someone we love. The memory of them mingles with the symbols of celebration, enriching those experiences of worship with a keen awareness that we have heard the Gospel because of the faithfulness of those who have gone before us, that we proclaim the hope of the centrality of Christ in our lives for those who come after us, that we manifest the miracles of love as the community of faith supports one another in their sorrow, their doubt, their joy – their Good Fridays and the Easter morns.

---Bettie Wilson Story

The following articles were written by Cullen Bryant Wilson, II for the church he pastored, Normandale United Methodist Church, Montgomery Alabama. These articles were written after his discovery of having a rare form of lymphoma in October of 1994. They follow his faith journey during most of the two years he travelled down the unwanted and difficult path of cancer and its' debilitating treatments.

Bryant's purpose was to be transparent with his family, friends and congregation during his emotional roller coaster ride of faith with an unwelcomed disease. He accomplished his goal and beyond as these articles ministered to all who read them and provided encouragement to those who could draw from them.

The purpose of this collection in book form is to provide readers with encouragement, empathy, compassion and faith to endure the hurdles that life sends to each and every one.

As you embark on this journey you will discover that Bryant passed the test of faith. Prayers over this work are that all readers will be drawn closer in their walk with God, that faith will grow in each soul, that spirits will be strengthened to endure each challenge faced and that God will be glorified.

--Pamela Woodham (Wilson) Ross

ACKNOWLEDGEMENTS

To those who have been thrust into the world of cancer, either as the patient, family member or friend. May you be encouraged through the "But if not" faith God provides.

This book is not one to be read as a novel. The intention of this compilation of articles is to be a source of encouragement and comfort to those whose lives have been touched by cancer and other trials of faith.

I couldn't have compiled this work without the writings themselves from my deceased husband, Cullen Bryant Wilson, II. For his honesty and transparency during his trial with cancer many have been comforted and blessed. Bryant's late sister, Bettie Wilson Story, provided necessary editing and organizational ideas.

This work has been a goal of mine for the past twenty years. The decision to finalize the dream came from a friend, Eva Langley, whose husband had his own battle with cancer. Her vision of how this could help others gave me the impetus needed to get started. For her encouragement I am eternally grateful.

Our children, Cullen, Natalie and Jessica, were a necessary source of support. Their Dad's ministry touched them deeply and they were eager for others to benefit from his faithful journey.

This entire effort could not have been accomplished without the patience and monumental support of my husband, Andy. We have been together for 19 years and his understanding and love during this process has proved invaluable.

I am grateful for the prompting of the Holy Spirit as I progressed from the first typed letter until the last. To God be the glory as lives are touched by His spirit.

DISCOVERY

The doctor called a day early. Wanted me to know the test results, he said.

My breath shortened. Quicker pulse. All ears. Grab the better phone. Sit down. "Yes sir."

"You may have a lymphoma," he said.
    He said other things, too:
"Ordering a CT Scan." "Appointment with an oncologist."
    (Is that a cancer, doctor?) Yes.
"More tests. Still not sure. But probably."

Stunned. Scared. Didn't Dad die of lymph cancer? Me, too?
    Awful news to hang up the phone and be alone with.

I was supposed to find out the next day when my wife of twenty years, Pam, could be with me.

    We would share it together.
        Hold each other if it wasn't good news.
            Rejoice together if it was.
    But instead I was …. alone.

A talk with my radiologist friend: "Oh, a lymphoma. Well, you're not ready to be buried yet!"

    Yesssssss! News I needed. A first ray of hope.
    It sometimes comes in small packages.

But, how do I share the discovery?
    How do I tell a wife who desperately wants, needs, the
        relief – the solace, of Good News?
            How? When? Where? What words?

Yet I find I want to keep it to myself. Keep it tucked away inside. Be stoic. Wait a day. Deal with it alone.

Make love to my wife without a sentence/a specter hanging over us.

The dam broke the next day when the family left for school and work. When I was left …. Alone.   Again.

On the bathroom counter I found the note that opened the gate.

A caring note left by my sixteen year old daughter said it all.
She did not know the Discovery, but the card simply read:

GOD BLESS YOU, FATHER.

Our Father watches over us,
    His children one and all.
No burden is too great for Him,
    No problem is too small,
For we are precious in His sight,
    And sheltered in His care.
Our Father watches over us.
    His love is everywhere.

…then she told me she loved me.
And that everything will be fine.

That is when the flood came –
    Falling to my knees on the bathroom floor;
    an anguished cry: NOOOOOOOOOOOOO!
    Non-stop. A morning of mourning.
    Raw emotion.
    Hours of anguished prayer. Calling out unto the Lord.
        (Can He, will He hear me?)
    Finally…exhaustion. And peace.

"Lord, if Faith and Hope and Love can heal, let it begin."

And then I was ready to share the Discovery.   *Bryant*

THERE IS A RIVER

There is a river, it is overflowing.
There is a river, it's a healing stream.
Let's go for cleansing in that river
That flows by the throne of God.

    He sits enthroned above the waters,
    Enthroned above the flood,
    Almighty God, Jehovah is He.
    O, the blood that flows through that mighty river
    Healeth even me.

There is a Savior, His name is Jesus
There is a Savior, He died for you.
In His arms he'll take and shield you
Give grace and take you home.

    He sits enthroned above the waters,
    Enthroned above the flood,
    Almighty God, Jehovah is He.
    O, the blood that flows through that mighty river
    Healeth even me.

There is a Spirit, He is strong and holy;
There is a Spirit, He'll comfort you.
He'll bear you up and carry you.
Give help in time of need.

    He sits enthroned above the waters,
    Enthroned above the flood,
    Almighty God, Jehovah is He.
    O, the blood that flows through that mighty river
    Healeth even me.

January 1995   *Bryant*

A HEALING ADVENTURE

"Cancer." The C word.

Not an easy word to type. Not an easy word to say.

All sorts of ugly images are created in my mind. You see them as clearly as I do: tubes, hospital beds, shaking heads, teary eyes, skinny bodies, bald heads – pictures of pain. We all have seen them. Some of us have experienced them – either personally or to someone we love.

The "C" word has left very few families untouched. It has cut its wake through my family; Dad died at 44 years young. It has perhaps cut through yours, too.

Now it touches me.

Cancer creates mental pictures; it also creates emotions.

> Fear.
> Uncertainty.
> Rage.
> Despair.
> Desperation.
> And more.

You cry. You deny. You want to bargain with God. Priorities Shift – some things just don't seem as important anymore (they probably should not have been important in the first place). You pray. Really pray. Agonizing prayer.

And then, once the tears are dry and the words said, another feeling finds its way to the home of your heart; almost like a single shaft of light that pierces a dark, foreboding cloud. A clear, radiant beam that reminds you that the sun is still shining up above the clouds.

It has a name: Hope.

Phrases and facts and faith begin to come together, like a giant collage. A mural upon a wall that slowly takes shape and form.

"60% cure rate."

                  Caring doctors.   Supportive family.
                      Cards and phone calls.
                              Prayer.   Lots of prayer.
                      God's word:
        "I am the God that healeth thee."

I guess God's word is the Last Word.

Chemotherapy begins Monday. I say, "Let the healing adventure begin."

Bryant

"HUGS ARE BETTER THAN DRUGS"

We've all heard those words. We've read them on bumper stickers; seen them printed in the paper.

Sometimes they take on flesh and blood – just like they did this past Sunday.

> Memories of Sunday abound;
> Tom's words, "Let me handle the closing. Trust me."
> Taking communion,   "The blood for our sins.....
> The body broken for our healing."
> Sarah's singing, "Because He lives, I can face tomorrow."
> Bobby's prayer, "Lord focus your healing power
> through us today."
> Kneeling with my wife and family.
> A loving congregation gathered around.
> Laying hands on. Tears of support and love.
> John's observation from the balcony,
> "The congregation formed a cross in the center of the sanctuary."
> And then healing hugs. Medicine for the soul.

Monday I started a regimen of chemotherapy. Fancy drugs with fancy names like, Cytoxan, Novantrone, Oncovin, Prednisone, (CNOP for short).

> Drastic measures.
> Tough side effects.
> Yet healing agents.

But not as healing and as powerful as all those hugs and the messages that came with them:

> "We love you." "Call on us."
> "We want to help." "We'll be here for you."
> "We're praying for you."

The Bible has a unique word for the Body of Christ, the Church.

It's a Greek word: "Asklepion." It means, "Healing community."
It worked on Sunday.

The results so far: no side effects (at all) from chemotherapy.

Hugs really are better than drugs. I just may not lose a hair of my head.

> Thank you for being an "Asklepion,"
> and for loving me and my family.
>
> *Bryant*

HITTING THE WALL

It's the point where the next step doesn't come. End of the line. No more energy. Suddenly running on empty and no reserve to reach down into.

The Wall.

It comes by surprise. You think, "All is well," and suddenly your throat tightens, your voice fades, and you enter a tunnel; a Reality Warp. Everything moves in, closes around you, and the phrase, "weak as a kitten," takes on new meaning. Helpless. Drained. Lights out.

Time to stop. No choice.

You want to fight it. Samson and Delilah come to mind. The Story says that after getting his unfortunate trim, he foolishly (pridefully) said, "I shall rise up as before." But strength was gone. Vanished. The Wall is like that.

Time to listen. Time to rest.

I have discovered that life with chemotherapy means hitting the wall from time to time. It means letting your body dictate. You don't call the shots any more. Your body speaks and you listen. You're at the mercy of forces working inside your cells making you well, bringing you the gift of healing.

Perspective: Chemical warfare against cancer means getting well, not getting sick. The disease is not destroying me, the cure is forcing me to rest.

> Maybe walls are not dead ends,
> or obstacles to remove,

or heights to attain,
or barriers to break down,
or blockades to destroy.

Maybe walls are just there to lean on. Resting places on the healing journey.

Thank God for walls.

He is my refuge, my wall.

Bryant

PSALM I

Praise the Lord!

    Jehovah, my Creator, knows me inside out. He knows all about me and how I think.

    He knows when I feel on top of the world.
        He knows when I am insecure and afraid.
            He knows when I am upset and discouraged.

    He knows when I do not have answers.
        He knows when I wrestle with conflicts.
            He knows when I am lonely and uncertain.

    He knows when I rejoice…and He rejoices with me.

    The knowledge of how much Jehovah knows about me is staggering; it blows my mind. It is wonderful. Amazing.

    Sometimes it is scary and unnerving.

        Why? Because He sees not only my actions,

    but my attitudes, motivations, and

        intentions….

            the inside stuff.

He knows when I am bluffing and when I am
    just flying by the seat of my pants.

He knows when I am not feeling particularly
	religious.

He knows what I'm going to do before I do it.

He knows when I get credit when no credit is due.
	But He also credits my account when no one else
	Is paying attention.

   Sometimes I want to run and hide, but He is around every corner. I can't get away from Him.
		...But I really don't want to.

Why? Because I know I belong to Him and that He loves me...
							even me.

There is great security in knowing Jehovah cares.

						Praise the Lord!

						Bryant

ON CHOICES

Choice.

It's an overwhelming word. A scary word.

It means I am responsible. A God-created moral free agent.
That's incredible!

        I can say "No." I can say "Yes."
            I can select priorities and number
            them one through ten.
                I can evaluate options.

      I can decide between alternatives.
          I can reason it out; figure the
          positives and the negatives.
              When I face a fork in the road,
                  I can take the High Road
                    ...or...

     It all means I am writing my own story. No second drafts.
No dress rehearsals.
        Just daily choices all the way.

     I don't want that kind of responsibility. Sometimes I wish
Someone else would make the choices, especially the hard ones.
But I can't get away from it – even if they told me what to do,
        I would still have to decide whether to
            do it or not.
                      It's up to me.

     Thought: I think one of the biggest choices (and hardest) is
the choice to live.

    Not just choosing to live
        because I'm scared of dying
But choosing to live
        because there's an ultimate reason to.
        A purpose. A plan.

When faced with a potentially life threatening disease (like I am) I could make the choice to give up. Throw in the towel. Call it quits. Fade away. Choose not to fight. Resign myself and accept no challenges. After all, many do just that.

But I have made another choice:

    To live and finish the journey.
    To discover the Plan.
    To take the gift and say "Yes" to God.

        No turning back.

It's a choice I can live with.

3/1/95

Bryant

THE PATH

Thanksgiving in the mountains and a long solitary trek along a foot trail.

                        No family. No friends.
                        Just me and God.

A time to reflect in solitude. It's good to be alone –unfettered. No conversation. No keeping up. Freedom to stop, delay. Even hide. Time to pray.

    It was one of those marked out trails that you can follow for miles; a Footpath marked by paint on tree trunks and tree limbs; color coded for the proper trail.

                A path to follow.
                A trail blazed.
                        A Map. Directions to a destination.
                              Confidence in strange territory.
        No option but to trust the trailblazer.

      Thought: What if there were no path-makers in life. Each person's journey forged from Square One.

                No color-codes. No symbols.
                No guidelines. No principles.
                    No one to show you the way to get there.
                    Every turn a question.
                    Every tree the same.
                    No way home.
                      Lost.

The path's journey was sometimes steep, sometimes level. It took me across streams and rugged terrain; by high places with endless views, through undergrowth and mud. A lot like life.

But always before me was the next marker, its brilliant color proclaiming:

"Herein is the way to go. Walk ye in it."
"Follow me." "Trust me."
"I'll lead you home."
                                        Security..

The path led me to an old mountain cemetery with gravestones over 100 years old. Families who had lived all their lives in those mountains. And many, many infants who died before reaching even a year old. No names on the markers, just last name and "infant." Sad.

Is this where our journeys all end?
Does life's path simply lead to death and anonymity

"Maybe," I thought.

But then it was time to leave. And the same path that had led to the old cemetery now showed me the way out and the way home. The path did not end there. The colored markers still said, "Follow me. I'll show you the way up and out."

I paused. Gave thanks to God for the Path to Life He provides. Gave thanks for Jesus, our Trailblazer. Rejoiced that our journey does not simply end at the graveyard, but leads us to it and through it.

                                   The Way of the Cross
                                   Still leads home.

                                   Bryant

WHO AM I?

Sometimes you think you have it figured out. After all, it seems to be a simple enough question.

> You know your name. Your strengths.
> You become comfortable in the rolls
> > you play – husband, father, career.
> You know your limitations and liabilities.
> > You know your incongruences
> > > And how to hide them.
> You can fake it well.
> You an even think you are in control.

But then, the unexpected occurs and the equation is shaken up.

It may be unwanted and unwelcome sickness (like mine). Or tragedy. Or reversal of fortunes. Or loss of job. Or divorce. Or being by-passed. Or losing someone important. Or giving up a cherished dream. Fill in the blank.......

> They all have a common element: grief.
> > Loss.
> > Change of status.

Suddenly new emotions and feelings wash over your soul and you Really aren't sure how to answer the question.
> You may realize you never knew how.
> > The old answers just don't work anymore.
> You are a stranger in a strange land.
> A foreigner on a distant shore.

--Disoriented. Alone. Afraid. Empty.

It's just not you. Or who you thought you were.
And you can't go back.

The challenge comes in answering the question, "Who am I?" without The new labels: The cancer victim. The divorcee. The job statistic. The widow. The loser.

These labels have a way of locking themselves in – of sealing your fate and your identity. They define the "new you" and offer no hope.

I become what I believe myself to be….
"As a man thinketh, so is he."

So, who am I?   I remember that despite my circumstances,
I am…
A Child of God.   More than a conqueror. Strong when
I am weak.   Blessed.   An overcomer.
And…
Loved.

3/15/95

Bryant

GOD'S 2 X 4

Cancer is like getting hit upside the head with a 2 x 4.
                               As in getting your attention.

    The story comes to mind of the man who couldn't get his new mule to budge. The mule's prior owner was called in and he immediately brought the mule to his knees with a 2 x 4 to the side of the head, saying, "You've got to get his attention first."

    Maybe God is like that, too. I don't like to think He is that way, but if I'm honest, I have to admit that sometimes (a lot of times) He doesn't have my attention.

    Discipline required.

    Perhaps there are many causes:
                        Complacency. Comfort.
                        Distractions.
                        Poor choices.
                            Resistance to growth.
                              Self-sufficiency.
                    You name it.......

    So, my Bible says God disciplines those He loves. It also says, "No discipline is pleasant while it is being applied." True enough.

    God's 2 x 4 can take many forms:
                        Anxiety. Restlessness. Depression.
                        Mid-life crisis. Divorce.
                        Failure. Hurt. Fear. Rejection.
                        Bitterness. Emptiness.
                        And even illness.
                              Whatever it takes.

God doesn't cause them; He just uses them. After all, He cares too much to Let us go. Or just watch us drift. I care about my children the same way (and sometimes I have just as much trouble getting their attention).

Some learnings from this time of "Discipline:"

--Inner strength and hope and assurance come from time alone with God.
--A wandering eye toward distractions comes from a wandering heart.
--The "best" can often be sacrificed for the "good."
--Good intentions don't count (Isn't the road to somewhere
                                paved with them?).

--There is no substitute for focus and intentionality.
--Meaning and purpose come from consistently making Right Choices.
--Spiritual growth only occurs when we reach down within:

                Discover our taproot.
              Get past the resistance.
                      Pay the price –Over and Over.

--Prayer and God's Word are the only drill bits that can get past
                            the bedrock of resistance.

        Not church attendance.   Not good books.
            Not great tapes.   Not the right experience.
      Not the right person.   Not the right activities.
          Not pleasure or peace of mind.

                                Just the basics.

It shouldn't take God's 2 x 4 to teach (and reteach) those things.

Bryant   But sometimes it does.
                                                          4/8/95

"HELLO, AGAIN"

It's like saying, "Hello, again," to yourself.

Just when you think chemotherapy is causing you to die a slow death and is making you into a permanent vegetable that has no energy, no motivation, and no ability to concentrate, you begin to discover the "real you" (if such a thing exists) all over again.

Chemo's effects begin to wear off just when you begin to think they would never do so. Then one morning you wake up feeling "kind of" normal. "You" have returned like an old friend who drops by for an unexpected visit.

Words like, "Relieved," "Glad," "Free," come to mind.

It is good to be yourself again. You feel like doing things in which you had lost interest or ability.

"Tennis, anyone?" "Walk in the park?"
Time to write that report, make that call,
prepare that lesson, play.
Go. Do. Enjoy.
"You" were lurking behind the effect of all
those chemicals all along.
Back to normal.
Whew.

But the days go by and the next treatment looms and you realize that you will probably say, "Goodbye" to yourself again for a while. You don't want it. In fact, You dread it. (Can I put it off by calling in sick to the doctor's office? Please?)

Then I remember, I am getting well, not sick. And I again put my trust in the doctor and his chemicals and face the loss of me...for a while.

Thought: just maybe the experience of chemotherapy is a microcosm of life...
and death ...itself.

> After all, we're dying a slow death.
> And the years begin to take their toll and we lose
> Interests and abilities and
> > ...Ourselves.
> "Oh to be young again," she said,
> when she meant, "Oh to be 'me' again."

And we know we are going to die one day (statistics tell us one out of one dies). We dread it and deny it. "Extinction" is a scary word. It means an ultimate loss
Of self.
> We can't handle the prospect.

But when, like putting our trust in the doctor and his healing chemicals, we put our trust in the Risen Christ who went through death and came out unscathed on the other side and says, "See, it's me! Trust me. I am the Way. Follow me,"

We can...

Take the risk, let go of ourselves, say, "Goodbye, "
only to say, "Hello, again."

    Go. Do. Play. Enjoy.
       It's you.

                                        Back to normal.
                                                  Whew.

Bryant

"HOW'RE YOU DOING?"

It's a question I get asked a lot.
    And the answer is not always easy -- it changes day-by-day.
    The easiest answer is, "Fine," or "Pretty good," or "Fair,"
    or can't complain." You know, all the standard responses
                                         that don't say much.

    But I know the question is asked by those who
genuinely care -- they want to know if I'm faltering and failing or
whether I'm facing this challenge and winning...or if they can help.

    Cards and notes are left in my mailbox every day that constantly
remind me that I have prayer partners in many places who stand with me
and my family. The concern, the cards, the calls all let us know...
                                          We are not alone.

    So I want to answer the question, "How're you doing honestly.
After all, it's an honest question. The caring concern behind it
demands more than just a superficial "Fine."

I am two-thirds through my chemotherapy treatment at this point.
I will finish in July. Then more tests will be run and I will go from there.
Personally, I'm counting on cure.

The two biggest problems I encounter are fatigue and low blood counts.
Both are a direct result of the treatments I am receiving. It's funny that
the Symptoms of getting well are worse than the symptoms of being sick.
The cure is worse than the disease.

            But I'll take the cure any day.

When fatigue hits, I just have to stop (see my article entitled, "The Wall"). I find it impossible to do much of anything and I am utterly exhausted. But it soon passes. Rest is the Rx.

When low blood counts hit (about two weeks following treatment) I am quarantined. That means no uncooked vegetables or fruits, no fresh flowers, no hospital or nursing home visits, no being with sick people -- just hiding out from lurking bacteria.

Overall, I am doing well. My energy is good and I exercise when I can. My appetite is good and I haven't lost a pound. My attitude is great because I "know in whom I believe, and I am confident that He is able..." I'm learning and growing and God is using this time of my life and this experience to teach me and test me.

>I just don't want to miss the lesson
>or fail the test.

A friend told me recently that I fit the profile of those who conquer cancer: good general health, good attitude, lots of love and support and prayer. If I fit the profile, it's because of you...

>Your prayers, your caring concern,
>Your encouragement, your support...

>Because of all that, I really am
>"Fine."

5/18/95

Bryant

"I HAVE ALL THE ANSWERS…"

It was said on an advertisement on television.
       Obviously an expert. Trained.
             An answer to any and all questions.
                          Just ask him.

    I often wish those were claims I could make. I wish that there were questions over which I did not have to struggle -- or put on a shelf entitled, "Awaiting Further Revelation." I wish I didn't have to say, "I don't know" so much.

    Oh, I have opinions; and ideas; and thoughts on different subjects. Some informed, some not. Some educated guesses, some pure speculation. Some reasoned out and thoughtful, others simply hogwash.

    The problem is some questions defy clear answers, and as my mother used to say, "The more I know, the less I understand."
               And, "The more I know, the more I
                      realize I don't know."

    The old man rocked for hours on his front porch without saying a word when suddenly he raised a finger and blurted out, "I think…" We waited expectantly. But rather than revealing a Profound Truth, he slowly settled back in his chair and said, "But then again, I just don't know." I feel that way many times.

      I wish it weren't the case, but often I grapple with
          Confusion, Uncertainty, Doubt.
               It's when answers don't come easily or quickly.
                   When I'm left ………………….wondering.

One of the easiest questions to ask, but hardest to answer is "Why?" In fact, it may be one of the first questions we ask, especially when we know there is no answer.

"Why do innocent people suffer?"
"Why is there war and selfish conflict?"
"Why is there disease?"
"Why do bad things happen to good people?"
"Why is this happening to me"

Good questions. But "Why..." defies an answer. Besides – no logic, no rationale, no explanation will satisfy.

Perhaps the secret of having all the answers is not in having the right answer, but in asking the right questions:

Not, "Why is there suffering"
But, "What can I do to help?"
Not, "Why is there war?"
But, "Where do I need to make peace?"
Not, "Why is this happening to me?"
But, "What am I learning?"

No, I do not have all the answers to all my questions. I am not the Great Pretender. I am not an expert on life, or love, or the "Why'..."

But maybe the answers are not all that important. Maybe wisdom is more important than knowledge. Maybe if I make any claim, it should be...

"I have all the questions..."

But then that's questionable, too.

Bryant   6/8/95

"CAGED UP"

July the Fourth. Independence Day. Time to celebrate freedom.

We have all kinds of ways of reminding ourselves that we cherish our independence:
fireworks, patriotic songs and music, waving the flag, trips, bar-B-que, and the beach all are traditional ways of celebrating out freedom. A free society is indeed a marvelous and wonderful gift of God.

But as much as we love our freedom, it can come out in some pretty selfish ways.

"Don't tell me what to do!"
"You can't make me!"
"I've got rights, you know!"
"It's not my job."
"Don't fence me in."
"I'll do what I want."

It's almost as if independence means no restraints, no restrictions, no limits, no commitments, no going the extra mile.

Just let me do my own thing.

Too bad life doesn't work that way.

I'm housebreaking dog #2 (Max) right now. I keep him caged up all night and when no one's home. He protested at first. He whined. He cried. But he soon learned I meant business.

Oh, the day is coming when the lesson will be learned and he'll enjoy his freedom, but for now, I'm doing him and me a favor. Hopefully, he'll know freedom...with responsibility. He'll not do his "own thing" on my carpet!

Our early civic lessons in school always taught us that great responsibility comes with great freedom. I believe that is true in the spiritual realm, too.

Paul wrote, "For freedom Christ has set us free." Not freedom to do our own thing with no restraints or restrictions, but freedom to love and serve God and love and serve others.

Maybe our love for God and, more importantly, His love for us is like a cage. "God's love constrains us," Paul also wrote. It keeps us from selfishly abusing our freedom.

Like my dog, Max, we have important (life-saving) lessons to learn.

Have you celebrated your "cages" lately?

6/29/95

Bryant

"PROMISES! PROMISES!"

It seems like almost every day I get something in the mail that tells me that I'm a lucky winner.

A Caribbean trip. A condo in Canada.
$50,000 cash.   20% discounts. $10,000,000   maybe.

They all urge me to "Call now!" Have my Visa card ready. Take the blue chip and place it over the "Yes! I want my prize" slot and match it with the green button and scratch off the whatever to see if I get my "Early Bird" reward and mail it in by 12:00 Noon tomorrow signed by my lawyer and banker.

Oh, brother. Give me a break!
All I want is a promise I can stand on.
No con. No come on.

My mother used to call me every other day convinced she had really won this time. Then I would ask her as I had so many times before, "Mother, is there the word, 'if' anywhere in the letter? (as in, 'You have won if the last four digits of your secret prize number match the as yet unidentified Grand Prize number to be drawn in November, 1999')." Then she would say, "No." But I knew it was there. Just another Bulk Rate empty promise.

Maybe I'm too cynical. Or too smart. Or maybe just afraid to get my hopes up. After all, I hate disappointment. Yet I really do want to believer that maybe I am, just this once, the Lucky Winner. But I know the odds.

For instance – last week's "losing numbers" in the Florida lottery:
1 through 162,489,612 and 162,489,614 through 999,999,999.

So much hope riding on empty promises!

34

But I want you to know that I'm the Lucky Winner. My number will come up. I'll take home the prize. The Prize: cancer cure.

Maybe I've stood and sung, "Standing On the Promises" one too many times. Maybe I've preached too many sermons on the "precious promises" of the Bible. Maybe I'm foolish enough to believe that faith can move mountains. Maybe all that preacher talk has gotten to me. Whatever. But I'm taking the chance and I'm not hedging my bets. Or bluffing. Deal me in.

I'm playing for Keeps.

7/5/95

Bryant

'THE NEWS'

OK, I admit it. I'm an addict. Hooked.

Every day between 5:00 and 6:00 P.M. I'll be found in front of Dan Rather or Tom Brokaw in order to find out what's happening in the world. I'll "channel surf" between ABC, NBC, CBS, and CNN just to keep informed. My wife knows not to have supper ready before 6:00 P.M. She knows that either I'll let it get cold or I'll eat it in front of the TV. Maybe you could call me a "News Junkie." I need my daily fix. From O.J. to Bosnia to the Dow Jones average to whatever...

During my bout with cancer I have often wished that I could get a daily report on my progress toward conquering it. I knew how I felt from day to day, but as far as knowing whether the chemotherapy, interferon shots and all the rest were destroying those wayward cells, I have had no idea.

It would certainly be nice to have a news headline daily that said something like:

2,317 CANCER CELLS DESTROYED!
SURE CURE IN THE WORKS FOR WILSON!
But it hasn't been that way.

Instead, it has been a journey of faith. You live with no news reports. No headlines. No special bulletins. No extra editions. No updates. Just hope. And hope is sometimes all you need.
But that doesn't mean it's been easy.

It means that you learn to live as an uninformed person. Concern and doubt and fear and uncertainty and anxiety can take over your imagination if it were not for the power of hope. Hope really does sustain us. And when the doubts creep into the crevices of your mind, you have to take a stand – a stand based on hope.

So for six months I have waited for the official news report. The informed word that would let me know the status of my personal war with cancer. Six months is a long time to wait for a "news junkie" like me – especially when the war is not a half-world away, but raging inside me.

So the news came yesterday: Clear.   No cancer.

John Robert McFarland, a United Methodist pastor and cancer conqueror put it this way: "For a cancer patient, negative is positive. The best news we can get is that there's nothing there. Our top grade is a zero." In other words, we hope that we fail our tests. I failed the test – nothing is there.

Now, next to the Good News I can't think of any news I'd rather hear.

Thank you for your faith, prayers, and hope.
They have made this news possible.

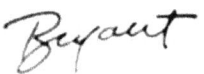

"A MOP-UP OPERATION"

"Then why am I taking additional chemotherapy treatments?"

It seemed like a reasonable question to ask of my cancer doctor. Especially since he had told me that there was no cancer present, and that my treatments had been effective.

"Well," he replied, "there are some —what we would call 'freckles' — we want to take care of. They are not cancer, and we all have them, but with your history we want to continue by giving you two more treatments."

Yuck! But I am, after all, a pragmatist. I'd rather be safe than sorry. And I'm enough of a hypochondriac that I don't need a few "freckles" keeping me up at night.

>Yes. I'll go along with the program.
>I'll do what I have to do.
>Call it a "Mop-Up Operation."

So, cancer is gone. Victory is mine. God is indeed a faithful healer. His promise is true.
Yet, there is work to be done.   Healing to continue.

I am reminded of a greater battle that all of us fight every day. It is a battle with the cancer of sin that eats away at our hearts and souls – and the soul of the world itself.

We see it all around us in many forms: War. Pride. Greed. Apathy. Hunger. Brutality. Death. Crime. You name it. It is a cancer that spreads its roots into every aspect of our lives. And its cure far more radical than the most vicious of chemotherapies – the death of the Son of God.

And His victory was complete. We sing, "Victory in Jesus," and "What Can Wash Away My Sin? Nothing but the Blood of Jesus." Scripture reminds us that, "For in Him all the fullness of God was pleased to dwell...making peace by the blood of His cross." (Colossians 1:19,20). Sin was defeated and destroyed by Christ.

Yet the unbeliever, the skeptic, the agnostic, the atheist has trouble at this point. He doesn't see it. He asks the same question I asked my doctor: "Why are we still fighting it?"

There is another verse of scripture we often ignore. It is found in Hebrews 2:8. It reads, "Now putting everything in subjection to Him, he left nothing outside His control. As it is, we do not yet see everything in subjection to Him. But we see Jesus, who for a little while was made lower than the angels, crowned with glory and honor because of the suffering of death, so that by the grace of God He might taste death for everyone."

Yes, the "freckles" of the cancer of sin are all around us...
Yet, the victory is complete.

What does it mean?

There is work to be done. Healing to continue.
Call it a "Mop-Up Operation."

Bryant

"HANG IN THERE"

It's advice that I receive all the time.

Oh, it may be a common cliché, but to me it is an encouraging reminder to

        Stay the course.   Don't give in.
               Don't give up.   Don't give out.

    It comes from people who know me and who love me. It comes from people to whom I am only a faceless name on a prayer list. It comes from people who are fighting their own battles...
        And need encouragement as much as I do.

    It comes as good advice from those who have been there; those who know that good rewards come to the ones who persevere. It is a testimony of victory for faith, hope, and keeping on keeping on.
        They're telling me: "It'll be alright."

    It comes from those who are fearful that discouragement, fatigue, or impatience may creep in the back door of my heart and eat away like dry-rot on the positive expectations of faith. They know how easy it is to look at the circumstances...and lose heart. Many of them know...
        They've been there.

    It comes from people who admire your courage and attitude; those who are silently and secretly observing how you handle the adversities that come in and scramble life's plans and dreams like breakfast eggs. They don't let you know you are a role model, and maybe they don't even know it yet. But they are watching.
        They don't want to see me fail...
        It's shared victory.

And even God himself says, "Fight the good fight," and tells me to put on the whole armor of God, that I might be able to "stand in the evil day, and having done all, to stand."

After the dust and rubble clear, I want to be left…

Standing.

Well, I'm almost at the end of my healing journey. My next test is Tuesday. To all those who have prayed with me and for me, who have believed with and stood by me, who have shared my journey and shared my faith, and who have encouraged me to, "Hang in there," I have only one message:

I'm hanging in there.

Bryant

"FOR ALL THE RIGHT REASONS..."

Have you ever done the wrong thing for the right reason?
Or the right thing for the wrong reason?

I have. I can think of many examples. Things I did because I had to and not because I wanted to. Mistakes that betrayed my true intentions. Failures for which I could always find excuses. Good deeds which masked questionable motivations. Good intentions which were never expressed in actions.

Paul said, "The good I want to do, I don't do. And the evil I don't want to do, I do." (Romans 7:15). Can you identify?

Of course.

I look over my own spotted history and it makes me truly appreciate the times that I did the right thing for the right reasons...the times I followed through...the actions that came from my heart...the times I lived up to the highest and best that I knew...the circumstances which could pass the test of scrutiny...when "Yes" meant "Yes" and "No" meant "No"...

It's called....
"Walking in the Light"
"Living by the Truth"
"Fleshing out the faith"
...It leaves me feeling good.

Prayers, Presence, Gifts, Service...Stewardship.

I don't want to...
Pray selfishly.
Attend only out of duty.
Give grudgingly.
Serve out of coercion.

I want to do the right thing for the right reason.

Why? Perhaps Edgar Albert Guest put the answer best in his poem, "Myself".
The first two lines begin:
> I have to live with myself, and so
> I want to be fit for myself to know.

His poem ends this way:
> I never can hide myself from me,
> I see what others may never see,
> I know what others may never know,

I never can fool myself – and so,
Whatever happens, I want to be
Self-respecting and conscience free.

> Maybe it's called,
> Stewardship of the Soul.

Bryant

PRAYER, HEALING & MIRACLES

What to pray...
How to pray...
What to expect...?

It's true. Prayer raises almost as many questions as it answers.

And I wish it came more natural. Unfortunately, I struggle with time, inclination, and moods which affect the quality and quantity of my prayers...and whether I pray at all.

Oh, I know God knows my heart and He knows my need even before I voice it to Him, but then I read about the prayer warriors who accomplish so much through their prayers and sometimes I feel guilty. After all, I find myself taking more time to read the morning paper than I do in devotions and prayer.

Like a lot of people, I find myself praying on the run – in the car or on the way out the door. I am not happy when a busy schedule gets in the way. But sometimes I can't blame busyness...
I wonder what I am avoiding.

I believe in the power of prayer. I have experienced the results of prayer. I know that healing and miracles and incredible results happen when we pray in honesty, sincerity and fervor. But I also find roadblocks to my prayer life that are hard to overcome.

It's true that Satan would probably have us do anything but pray. It is a spiritual battle that we fight even to take time to pray.

Am I describing you, too? Perhaps I am.

If I am describing you then I invite you to be a part of our Sunday evening study on prayer and miracles. It will go for 8 weeks and my prayer is that we all may gain both wisdom and knowledge that will enable our prayer life to become easier, more natural, and more powerful.

I am ready to see God move…in the world, in my church, in my family, but most important…in me.

Bryant

DOING THE GROWN UP THING

I don't like being a grown up.

Oh, it's not that I don't enjoy all the benefits of what it means to be on my own, and responsible for myself. It's just that a kid isn't expected to take things seriously. The grown-ups do that.

Grown-ups do the worrying. They do the hurrying. They get involved in things like politics and the stock market. They pay the bills. They fret. They sweat. They concern themselves with things like debt. They have to make the tough choices.

Kids can take it easier.
They can let the big people handle all those things.

Discipleship and stewardship are some of those grown-up words I wish I could avoid. They involve tough choices. They ask me to be responsible...not only for myself, but for God, too.

They force me to get serious...
Ask difficult questions.

Then there are all those Bible stories that make me have to think. They make me look at myself. The kid in me does not want to think or take a look at myself. Those stories I like to avoid involve being a good steward, a wise planner, a faithful servant, a committed disciple. Grown-up stuff.

Paul said, "When I was a child, I talked like a child, I reasoned like a child. When I became a man, I put childish ways behind me." (I Corinthians 13:11). I wish it were that easy for me. No, it's not easy...but necessary.

My mother always said to me when I was growing up and wanting to be my own boss and do my own thing, "Responsibility comes with freedom." I liked the "free" part –not the "responsible" part.

Mom was a good teacher – even if I didn't like what I was taught.

Well, whether I like it or not, I'm a grown-up now. The lessons about stewardship and discipleship that I would like to avoid provide me a lot of freedom at the same time. I know that now.

And I am free…free to be me, free from guilt, free from sin, free to make God's will, my will.

On Loyalty Sunday, November 12, I want to say, "If it's God's will…I will."

After all it's the grown-up thing to do.

Bryant

"CAN I GO TO DISNEYLAND INSTEAD?"

It seems like a fair question.

After all, spending seven days in a Mobile hospital is not exactly my idea of the ideal Christmas vacation. I.V. drips, raging temperatures, and general misery are not equal to a trip to the Magic Kingdom in my book.

But, let's face it – the unexpected and unwanted often happens., Right when we least expect it or need it. At those times, it is important to remember that the God of peace and joy is also the God of comfort and healing; the God of blessings is also the God that delivers; the God that promised, "I will be with you," means it both in the good times and the not-so-good.

I will face some difficult and important decisions over the next few weeks --unwanted and unwelcome decisions I would rather not have to make. Decisions regarding extensive treatments and massive amounts of chemotherapy what's ahead. My week in the hospital was only a possible taste of what is to come if I have to proceed with treatment.

Disneyland is not part of the Rx.

But I know that my God, my church, my family and my friends will be with me. I know that I will make the right decisions and that everything will turn out as God plans.

I need you and we need each other. That's how God works. He knew that life is not always lived in a theme park, and when the hard times come, we have one another to lean on, look to, and love.

Yes, I would rather go to Disneyland. But it's OK. The ride I take may be bumpier than any I would find there, and not near as much fun. But this I know: Faith and Hope and Love will sustain you no matter what you have to face – and they will sustain Bryant Wilson.

And that's not just "Mickey Mouse" stuff.

1/4/96

Bryant

"THE SKINHEAD BLUES"

Well, I hoped it would never come to this.

A shaved head, that is.

However, chemotherapy has finally accomplished its work and I now look like a plucked turkey. Losing hair by the handfuls over the last few days seemed like too long a process, so I gave in to the inevitable and got a "trim".

Believe me, Yul Brynner, Kojack and Montel Williams have nothing on me now -- neither does my head. And Winter time is not the best season for this experience. Pam suggested we make Sunday "Hat Sunday", but I don't think that's necessary. And if my new fashion statement starts a trend, well, my barber will be glad to help you out. But as I look around, many of you gentlemen have already been to see him — or at least it seems that way. Maybe I'm the one behind the times.

Thought: Scripture says man looks on the outward appearance but God looks on the heart. I'm truly glad he looks on the "inner man," especially these days. After all, we can change our outward appearance, get our hair cut or colored, wear our best clothes, and change out looks – but that doesn't change our hearts.

Only Christ can do that.

After all, He changes us from the inside out -- the way it really counts. I may have a new look, but what I want (and need) is a new heart.

Well, it may take a while for me to get used to my "new look" in the mirror, and it hopefully won't be forever. But the change Jesus brings about is eternal, and I want to be wide open for the "trim work" He wants to do in my life.

His is a "scalping" process I won't mind.

Bryant　　　　　　　　　　1/11/96

I'VE GOT SOMETHING TO SAY...

Or, better said, God has given me a word.

This coming Sunday is the first Sunday in Lent. As you know, Lent is a season of spiritual growth, reflection and examination. Prayers, penitence, and self-denial mark the season as we prepare to rightly celebrate the power, glory and joy of the Resurrection. The cross stands before us....

For me...it's different this year.

Though all the above is true for me, this year I find not only the cross before me, but also one of the most unwanted, unwelcome, unexpected and unpleasant experiences of my life -- bone marrow transplant at UAB in Birmingham. Yuck.

Unfortunately, as the schedule stands now, if I am indeed deemed a candidate for this procedure, I will go to Birmingham the first week in April with weeks of recovery following. My disappointment is that I will miss sharing Palm Sunday, Holy Week and Easter with you. These eight days are the pinnacle of the gospel celebration – there is no other like them.

So, what I say I must say...now.
...and God has given me a Word.

I have shared with you in worship over the past two weeks about coming to church with an expectancy about what God will do or say, and how He might manifest Himself to us and display His presence...the Glory.

I challenged us to examine whether the modern church in American has lost her sense of expectancy and become like Jesus' hometown of Nazareth where he could do no miracles because of familiarity, unbelief and low expectation.

What I believe God wants me to share with you over the next few weeks involves the key to the kind of expectation that brings forth God's blessings, healings, divine presence and miracles.

I urge you to be present.

God has spoken to my heart.

Bryant

"IN LIMBO..."

Stuck. Yeah, that's the word.

Have you ever been there? Waiting. No decision. Awaiting further info. Nowhere Ville, USA. Wondering. Worrying.
                    You probably know what it's like.

We've all been there at some point or other in our life. It's the time when no answers are forthcoming, all roads seem to lead to a dead end, and no action can be taken. It can be frustrating at best, maddening at worst.

I find myself living at that address right now. Trips to the hospital, inconclusive tests, waiting for treatment decisions, and delay have taken their toll. It happened again this week – sent home from the University Hospital in Birmingham. More tests needed. More options need consideration.

Oh, it's not that I don't appreciate them taking the time to make sure they make the right decision. But to be honest, I'm emotionally wrung out, tired. Scared. Sometimes I feel very vulnerable and little...like I'm somebody else's property and they are in control.

        Sometimes I want to run away and hide...
          Or say, "Stop the world, I want to get off."

But then a caring phone call comes along out of the blue and the voice on the other end says, "We love you. We're praying for you. Hang in there." The unexpected card the postman leaves in my mailbox that says, "It'll be OK. Don't give up," seems to come at the right time. God's timing is amazing.

And then the devotional "Thought for the Day" seems to be written for me (how did the editors know to put it on the day I would need it most). It reminds us to "stand firm," "persevere, and most importantly, "trust."

Living in Limbo is not easy, but reminders that while I'm there, caring thoughts, prayers, and love are surrounding me make all the difference in the world. I'm reminded too that even when things seem stuck in limbo, God is still on the throne and my life and times are in His hand.

After all, Limbo is not forever.

Bryant

"WASHED OUT BUT NOT UP"

A poem I learned long ago reads:

> "The best laid plans of mice and men
> Gang aft agley. (Old English for "go awry")
> And leave us naught but grief and pain
> For promised joy."

I have (again) learned the meaning of those words. Despite the well-made plans, the detailed calendar of tests and procedures, and the ordered schedule provided by the UAB Hospital, they are cancelled. There will be no bone marrow transplant. I am not a candidate.

The first emotions are disappointment, unbelief, fear, depression, even anger.

> Washed out.
> A source of hope removed.
> A door closed.
> A means of escape denied.

And questions. Lots of questions. Like, "Where do we go from here" "What happens next?" "Where (and to whom) do we turn?" "Should we give up?" "Can I take any more?"

Conversations follow. With doctors, friends, family…and with God. And unexpectedly, that God-given shaft of light called "Hope" breaks through again. Words of hymns begin to float across the window of my mind:

> "A mighty fortress is our God, a bulwark never failing.
> Our helper He amid the flood of mortal ills prevailing."

> "Joyful, joyful, we adore thee, God of Glory, Lord of love;
> Hearts unfold like flowers before thee, opening to the sun above.
> Melt the clouds of sin and sadness, drive the dark of doubt away;
> Giver of immortal gladness, fill us with the light of day!"

"He leadeth me: O blessed thought. O words with heavenly comfort fraught! What'er I do, where'er I be, still 'tis God's hand that leadeth me."

                                                  And more.

And I learn the lesson again: Trust. Hope. Believe.

Good Friday is coming. And life has its Good Fridays.

                              But hang On…Easter's not Far Behind.

                                                        3/28/96

Bryant

"HE LIVES..."

"I serve a risen Savior, He's in the world today
I know that He is living, whatever foes may say."

The joy of the Christian faith is indeed contained in these two lines...

Think of it! An empty tomb. A living Savior. Nor more fear of death. Because He lives we can live also. Resurrection!

Victory in Jesus!

Paul wrote in I Corinthians that if Christ did not rise from the dead than preaching is useless, our faith is in vain, we are false witnesses about God, and we are still in our sins. More than that, Christians are to be pitied above all other people.

But then he states, "But the fact is that Jesus did rise from the dead." How did he know? He met Him on the road to Damascus and Paul's life was forever changed.

And it has been the testimony of millions of people over the past 2000 years that this living Jesus has changed their lives as well.

Yes, we can live with the firm conviction that Jesus did rise from the dead...not because of the biblical record, the story of the empty tomb, the witness of the disciples following His death and resurrection, the witness of Paul or anything else, but because the Spirit of God bears witness to the Truth.

"How do I know He lives? He lives within my heart." That's the bottom line.

I hope to see you Sunday as we celebrate in song, witness, word, and spirit that Jesus is alive and living in the lives of those who receive Him and declare Him Lord.

Yes! An empty tomb is Cause for Celebration!

Bryant

April 11, 1996

"A Second Chance…"

I've always heard that God is a God of "second chances."

…That He never gives up.
…That He is always willing to let us start over.
…That He provides a way when we think the door may be shut.

Once again, I have found that to be true. God is faithful to His promise.

Due to the keen observation of a trusted radiologist friend, UAB in Birmingham has reconsidered me for a bone marrow transplant. I got the news yesterday. I will enter the hospital for treatment on April 18. According to the doctor, short of spontaneous remission, this treatment is the only chance I have for cure. Still no guarantees, but a chance. That's all I want or need.

It is a chance I'm willing to take.

However, it is not a chance without risks. One doctor told me, "Before now you have been hit with a fly swatter, you're getting ready to be hit with a MX missile." Oh, boy! I can't wait.

I will be out of the pulpit for several weeks. This Sunday will be my last for a while. But I know that I leave the pulpit, the office, and the ministry of the church in vary capable hands – Tom, Davis, Vykki, Susan, Homer – your staff. They are committed to making sure that things continue as they should.

But beyond them, there is you – the laypeople of the church. You are the ones who I really count on. Your willingness to be ministers of the church and to carry out and follow God's call upon you is what makes this a great church. If I have done my job effectively, it will be measured by your willingness to be used of God to carry out the work of the church. My job is to inspire, encourage, and equip you to be "Ambassadors for Christ."

My family and I know that we will be in your prayers, thoughts, and hearts. We have felt your love and support throughout this entire ordeal, and we know that you will continue to be there for us.

Let me say to you, I regret all this. I do not want to leave you. I do not want to be away from this church family, nor do I want to put the church through my problems or my absence. But I have no choice. Thank you for understanding and loving and providing God's grace during this agonizing and uncertain time.

I have been given a second chance. The door was shut, but God has opened it again. Prayer works and I am claiming God's healing promise.

>   If God isn't going to Give Up…
>   I'm not either.

Bryant

May 30, 1996

DAY BY DAY...

Day 52.   Day 109.   Day 87.

You hear references like this all the time at the bone marrow transplant unit at UAB. They are made by veterans of the transplant procedure as their recovery B.M. process continues. It is a reference to the number of days since the actual transplant took place.

For some, the recovery process is slow and uncertain. Others seem to skate through recovery as though it were a hang-nail problem.

Me?............Slow, but steady.

But looking at the big picture, I have gone through a most difficult and rough experience, No fun. I have lost 30 pounds, my skin is peeling off because of chemo, the small amount of hair which existed is long gone and I'm running on 1 ¼ mouse power. Does this sound like a picture portrait you would like to send home to mom?

And besides, I'm only on day 37. Just a novice.

Prayer, belief, and faith have carried us through. You have carried us through. God has carried us through.

I'm glad to be home. Recovery will be slower than I want, energy will not always be there when I need or want it, and I may seem to be "out of it" more than usual, but I'm glad to be home.

Why? Because the God of Day 1 will be the God of Day 40; and He'll be the God of Day 68; the God of Day 188; the God of Day 2,811; the God of Day....well, you get the picture....the God of Forever.

He made this day and all that will follow, and wants us to trust Him day by day....

So I guess I will....starting with Day 37.

Bryant

June 13, 1996

"WHAT NOW....?"

It was one of the first questions I asked my doctor.

Simply surviving bone marrow transplant treatment is one issue; recovering is another. Recovery for me is just as much of an unknown as anything else, and I have a need to know what to expect as much as I need to know anything.

Questions like: "How long?" "Am I cured?" "When can I go back to work?" "What symptoms should I look for?" Where can I go?" "What should I avoid?" "When will I get my strength back?..."

I have a list of questions a mile long.
Many, if not most, have no answer.

But a few things I do know.

On <u>Process</u>: Now is the time for monitoring. Watching closely. Being careful. Begin looking for that 5-year mark (remission for five years is Called cure in the medical profession). Rest.

On <u>Cure</u>: No guarantees. I have increased my odds of being cured, but no promises are given. Prayers are still needed and faith needs to be stronger than ever.

On <u>Strength</u>: A year. But stronger every day.

On <u>Work</u>: 3-6 months before I can work a 40 hour week. Several weeks. before I can be back in the pulpit.

<u>Things to Avoid</u>: Crowds. Sick People. Strenuous activity.

The Healing Adventure in many ways has just begun, and patience is not one of my virtues when it comes to getting well. I want to be well now and I want to know the future. Both impossible.

During my stay at UAB I always had before me a wall poster Pam had purchased. It is a picture of a gravel mountain road that twists and turns through the forest. Inscribed upon it are the words –

> "Never be afraid to trust an unknown future
> to a known God."

That is a reminder that you and I need every day. Trust in a loving God gives us faith for the future. When you know God, you know that He has "you and me Brother, in His hands."

No, I do not know all the answers and I do not have a crystal ball. But, it doesn't matter. I have a friend who will never leave me nor forsake me. He'll help me face the future.

It's Good to Know I Have a Friend.

Bryant

June 20, 1996

RESURRECTION

The doctor tried to explain the bone marrow transplant procedure to me.

He said, "The medicine we're going to give you (Bulsulphan) is guaranteed 100% to kill your bone marrow." "Oh?" I said, as if this were something that I was supposed to look forward to. "In fact," he went on, "We'll bring you to the point of death, but keep you alive until you recover enough to go home. Just sign here to give us permission to move ahead with the procedure."

Then my shaky hand scrawled out my name on his permission form. I doubt it's readable. After all, what was I giving him but permission to kill me (5-10% of people never make it through the treatment). I was literally putting my life in the doctor's hands. Could he deliver? What if he couldn't……?

Serious and risky business. But the decision had been made. Full speed ahead. Go for it. After all, it was my only chance. No turning back now.

A Gethsemane decision.
"Take me now before I change my mind."

The nest six weeks proved him right. In fact, there were at least two times that Pam felt that she might have to call in the family because it did not look like I would make it. There are two and one-half weeks of which I have no memory. "That's OK," Pam said, "There are some things you just don't need to remember."

I guess God takes care of us that way. He just erases the memory bank.

But then – Resurrection. Slowly, but surely, life returned. Awareness began to make a comeback. Consciousness and memory began to emerge. There were doctors and nurses – and my wife – waiting to greet me. They had pulled me through. Prayers had been answered. Hope was given its reward.

>Gethsemane.   The Tomb.   The Sunrise.
>New Life.

It's really the story of the Christian faith: Trust and Surrender ("Take me now"), Death ("I have been crucified with Christ"), and Resurrection ("We have been raised with Christ").

There really is new life on the Other Side. Hope sees it. Faith believes and receives it. Love assures it. Joy expresses it.

I'm glad to be alive. Now…..

And forever.

Bryant

June 27, 1996

RE-ENTRY

Did you see the movie Apollo 13?

It is the true story of our astronauts being stranded in space and having to re-enter earth's atmosphere on nothing but ingenuity and guesswork. It is a real-life drama that captured the world's attention twenty-five years ago. To re-enter they had to come in at the right speed, the right angle, the right entry point – all while running out of oxygen and fuel and without instrumentation or good ground communication. Our nation held its breath.

Timing – Faith – Luck – Skill – and answered prayer finally brought our astronauts to a safe ocean splash-down. The world rejoiced in their victory.

As my strength and stamina return and I prepare to re-enter Real Life, I realize the importance of timing –

>Not going too fast
>Not too slow
>Not getting ahead of myself
>Setting proper priorities
>Taking a day at the time
>Learning patience with my limitations
>Easing back into the atmosphere of schedules and responsibilities
>   deadlines and the "Must-Do's."

I admit, it scares me a little. My confidence crumbles as I ponder tough questions: Where do I begin? How much should I tackle? What's the right speed, angle, and entry point? What's expected? How much is too much?

Then I remember. I have all I need to land safely: Support. Experience. Prayer. A caring congregation. Wise counsel. Plenty of help. A wife with a sharp eagle eye on her husband lest he begin to take on too much.

And most importantly: A faithful Lord who desires to give guidance if I'm open.

A soft landing awaits. Soon I will be back with you...

And I Rejoice.

Bryant

July 18, 1996

"FROM SCRATCH..."

Are you familiar with that term? You should be.

It's how Grandma used to make biscuits until "Bisquick" came along. It means, "from the very beginning," or, "starting with nothing but the bare essentials." I guess its literal meaning is, "From the time you are standing there scratching your head, wondering what you are going to do."

If you have a better definition, let me know.

I like to think of God creating the heavens and the earth "from scratch." After all, the Bible says, "In the beginning...when the earth was without form and void." And He did a good job. I spent the Fourth of July at my friend's new home overlooking Lake Lanier in North Georgia. As we admired the beauty of the moon glistening across the water one evening, one of our discussions centered on the miracle of creation. God started "from scratch" and made a beautiful world! A paradise teeming with all kinds and shapes and forms of life. Wow!

"From scratch."

Since going through bone marrow transplant procedures I have begun to think that is what I am being made from. New hair, new skin, new fingernails, new cells throughout my body. I am being "remade" from nothing but the bare essentials. I thank God that He made our bodies with the capacity to heal and be renewed.

But, you know, I need more than just a new body. I need a new way of thinking...about God, about myself, about others.

A new Perspective...
A new Outlook...

A new way of seeing the world.
In short, a new Spirit.

Good News! God has made provision for that, as well. He says in His Word, "I will place a new spirit within you," and "Behold, I make all things new," and "Anyone in Christ is a new creature...the old has passed away." He also tells us to be "renewed in the spirit of our mind."

If being "Born Again" means anything, it means a change in thinking and perception that is so radical it is as though we were starting all over again, being made "from scratch."

Sometimes I picture God up in heaven scratching His head, trying to figure out what He's going to do with me. He doesn't have much raw material to work with, but it's a relief to know that whatever turns out will be "in His image..."

...hopefully, His love, His grace, His character.
After all, He knows how to scratch where it itches.

Bryant

Aug. 14, 1996

WINNERS AND LOSERS

I hate to lose.

Yep. I admit it. I'm competitive. Oh, I've learned to lose graciously, but it's still a lousy feeling. I guess I've been on the losing end enough times to be able to sympathize and empathize with the losing team. Think about it – for the few athletes who went back to their countries carrying an Olympic gold, silver, or bronze medal, thousands went home emptyhanded.

> They had worked just as hard...sweated just as much...
> Dreamed just as big...hoped just as heavily...
> And put out their very best.
>
> It just wasn't good enough.

For the glory that we shared with a few, there were boxcars full of disappointment, grief, and failure for the others. We saw the tears of victory trickle down the winner's faces. We never saw the oceans of tears flow down the faces of the also-rans. I want to remember them, too. They are heroes, all.

Linus ran excitedly up to Charlie Brown and said, "You should have been there, Charlie Brown! Our team won in the last few seconds of the game! Everyone went wild! We were yelling and screaming and running around hugging one another. They climbed the goal posts and tore them down. You should have been there!"

And Charlie Brown answered, "But what about the other team? How did they feel?"

As Christians, we are called and challenged to: "walk a mile in the other man's moccasins;" To see things through other's eyes; To identify with the poor; To bear one another's burdens; To reach out to the losers in life as much (if not more) as we applaud the winners.

Today, there is an elderly widow who hopes the phone will ring.
   Today, there is home-bound person who desperately wants a visit.
      Today, there's someone who feels neglected and unwanted...and unloved.
     Today, there is someone who will walk away from the mailbox
                                          emptyhanded.

                                      Many feel like losers.

    You can make a difference.

    A call. A visit. A card. A prayer.
                Little things that make us all winners.

                            Bryant

Aug. 29, 1996

Be At Rest Once More, O My Soul

> Be At Rest Once More, O My Soul,
> For the Lord has been
> Good to you.
> Psalm 116:7

I don't know about you, but my soul needs a good talking to sometimes.

Yes, it's true, I need reminding. After all, it's a part of the faith process.

> Reminding.   Remembering.
> Recalling.   Reflecting.

I especially need it after a setback, a disappointment, or when I'm "all shook up". I need to be reminded of God's goodness to me in the past and the times He answered when I called on Him.

You see, my spirit-man knows I can and should rejoice in the bad times, but it's my soul – my thoughts, my imagination, my wandering will – that give me the restless nights and the worried frown. I mean, God may have answered my earnest plea yesterday, but what about today? Has He forgotten me? What if it's too late? Does He have more important persons and problems to deal with? What if He's mad with me?

> Oh, the obsessing of
> an unanchored soul.

Time for my spirit-man to come to the rescue. Time to drop anchor again and review the basics: He knows me. He loves me. He is here now and will never leave me. He is able. And willing.

It all begins with reminding myself how God has come through in the past. The time my back was against the wall and He provided a way out. The friend He sent just in the nick of time. The financial breakthrough when I was broke. The prayer that was answered when I least expected it. The divine coordinates He used in working out my life's plan and purpose. The healing hand He placed upon me. The marvelous power of hope engendered within my heart when it looked as though all was lost.

Yeah! Listen up, soul. The Lord has been good to you. What more proof do you need? Take that, doubt and confusion – be gone. Soul, be at rest again.

Are you down? Discouraged? Fed up? You may want to read all of Psalm 116. It's a great reminder.

Yes, I need a good talking-to from time to time.

After all, it's better than being taken
behind the woodshed.

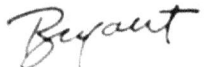

September 12, 1996

TUG OF WAR

"Teach me your way, O Lord, and I will walk in you truth;
Give me an undivided heart, that I may fear your name."
Psalm 86:11

Confused. Uncertain. Double-minded. Wish-wash. Reed-in-the-wind. Indecisive. Mr. Can't Make Up My Mind.

Ever been there? Sure you have. Me, too.

I especially feel that way when I don't know all the facts. Information black-outs always leave me in Nowhereville. And when I want to please everybody I have a tendency to play the middle-of-the-road. And when the commitment has to be up front or when the down-payment is high, I can get real indecisive…
"I really would like to, but you see….."
Fill in the blank.

I can be that way about little things, too. I've been known to walk around a Baskin-Robbins for 30 minutes and finally get vanilla. It seems like there's always a Tug-of-War going on about something.

And it's true spiritually, too. I know God's promises but I often have to be reminded. I guess that's why when I preach…
I'm preaching to me, too.

The Tug-Of-War is a battle between fear and faith, despair and hope, grief and joy. When I find myself "sitting on the premises," instead of "standing on the promises" I have a decision to make. I've got to decide what side of the rope I am going to pull. I can't be wishy-washy anymore.

I have to take a stand and pull hard.

And that's when one obscure promise in God's Word comes in handy. It says God will uphold us with His mighty Arms. In this Tug-of-War…

I Can Use an Extra Set of Arms.

Bryant

September 18, 1996

TIGHTROPE

I walk a tightrope. And I dare not look down.

I assume that most of you have heard the discouraging word that I received from my doctors this past week. Despite their best efforts, and mine, and yours, the cancer we would wish away and pray away has returned. It's nobody's fault. It just is...

And now I walk a tightrope.

As I hang precariously balanced I find keeping balance is not easy to do. On one side is the reality that all of us die, even young men in their early 50's. Cancer is not a respecter of persons. It can take us all....
    The Young and the Old.
        The Rich and the Poor.
            The famous and Infamous...
    Those that some would think deserve it
            And those that don't.   And me.

Denial is only foolish.

And on the other side is Faith. The kind of faith that knows miracles can and do happen. God can and does intervene. Prayers are miraculously answered. Bodies are healed. Lives are restored. Cancers are banished and vanish...

    Without explanation. Unpredictably.
    Wonderfully.

Denial refuses the Unseen Mystery of life.

To own both realities is difficult. It is easy to embrace one and deny the other – to accept death and deny hope; to cling to faith and deny death.

I live on a tightrope. Balance can get shaky. But I know that, were I to fall, it matters not what side I fall on. Faith always wins and I am guaranteed a soft landing. Why?

Underneath are the Everlasting Arms.

Bryant

BATTLEGROUND

"For our struggle is not against flesh and blood,
But against the rulers, against the authorities,
against the powers of this dark world and against
the spiritual forces of evil in the heavenly realms.
Ephesians 6:12

I go to battle every day.

The problem is that mine is an unseen enemy. Maybe yours is, too.

It is a battle fought in the mind. Instead of bombs, guns, tanks, and bullets, the arsenal the enemy uses against me comes in the form of thoughts, ideas, and imaginations. Just when I need something to go right, the car breaks down. Boom! Discouragement has just been lobbed from over the next hill. Just when I think I'm getting better, the doctor's lab report states that ain't necessarily so. Bang! A hidden landmine of doubt goes off under my feet.
Pray for relief and pain gets worse.
Look to God for answers and nothing comes.
Dead ends. Closed doors.
It's a War on Faith.
A battle in the heavenly realm.

Then the small artillery starts coming from all directions. Thoughts like "Where is God?" "Do you really think He wants to heal you?" "You're probably going to die." "What's the use?" and "What good is belief and prayer?" begin to bombard the serene quiet of my bunker of faith.

Have you ever been caught in the crossfire? Sure you have. You've fought the same battle. We all share a common enemy. His tactics are universally the same. He uses circumstances, disappointment, defeat, hurt, bitterness, resentment, sickness, anxiety – you name it – to produce confusion and doubt. The War on Faith is daily and relentless. Casualties abound.

Well, thank goodness, I'm not left defenseless. Ephesians 6:8 goes on to describe the protection and weapons afforded us: The Belt of Truth, the Breastplate of Righteousness, the Helmet of Salvation, the Sword of the Spirit, the Shoes of the Gospel, Prayer. It's called the Armor of God.

And verse 16 states, "In addition to all this, take up the Shield of Faith, with which you can extinguish all the flaming arrows of the evil one."

I may be under attack, but no matter….
                                                      The Victory is Mine.

Bryant

October 22, 1996

"BUT IF NOT..."

They are the most powerful words of faith in the Bible.

The three Hebrew children are prepared to be turned to soot and ashes as they ready themselves to be thrown in King Nebuchadnezzar's fiery furnace because they refused to bow down to a false god, a mere image of gold.

They knew there is only one true God. No substitutes, please.
No matter what the cost. In this case, a toasty end to their young lives.

Let's listen in on their conversation to the king. They pull no punches. They tell it like it is. "If we are thrown into the blazing furnace, the God we serve is able to save us from it, and He will rescue us from your hand, O king. But even if He does not, we want you to know that we will not serve your gods or worship the image of god you have set up."

Now that is an "if not" kind of faith. The kind of faith I want. No sinkers No sliders.
        Just straight, hard, and fast.

You see, faith is not faith unless it has passed the test of not getting what it wants.
    "If not" faith can handle it when God says, "No."
        The unhealed body.
            The untimely death.
                The divorce that came anyway.
        The promised promotion that turned out to be
                an empty promise.
    The friend who misunderstood anyway.

The list goes on and on........

In order to handle disappointment, frustration, or failure it takes an "if not" faith. When it's not there, it just means a "Fair Weather" faith that does not hold when the winds and rains of adversity and unanswered prayer come howling against it.

Well, I am faced with dying or living. I am confident I serve a healing God who is able, and willing, to deliver me. But as the flames lick higher and the temperature surges, I pray for an "if not" faith. Job said it, "Though he slay me, yet will I trust him."

That's the kind of faith where you don't get burned...regardless.

Bryant

Rev. Cullen Bryant Wilson, II

(1945-1996)

C. Bryant Wilson was born on May 9, 1945 and died October 28, 1996.

Bryant's life and ministry were all too brief in terms of years, but the depth and quality of his ministry were beyond measurement.

The Gospel to Bryant was God's Good News and he proclaimed it from the pulpit, with eloquent writing, and in his daily life. His life of faith matched his proclamation.

Bryant was devoted to his family. The Wilson name is prominent in the history of the Alabama-West Florida conference of the United Methodist Church. Bryant faithfully carried the mantle of a ministry borne by his father, uncles and cousins.

He loved the United Methodist Church. He believed in her mission and message. He faithfully discharged his duties as a loyal minister.

Bryant was truly a dedicated man of God.

Cullen Bryant Wilson

Servant of God, well done.

Thy glorious warfare's past,

The battle's fought,

The race is won.

And thou art crowned at last.

A place called...

NEUTRAL...

You know the place...
    No movement forward or back...
        Idling, engine running, waiting for direction...

I learned to drive my Papa's old blue, standard shift Buick. The man had the patience of Job, or at least I though he did. There's no telling what stories he told others of my learning experiences with that old car. Lurches forward and back, engine dying with cars waiting behind, sweaty palms, tight throat...
    All part of getting the "hang of it" he would say.

I spent a lot of time in neutral learning where each gear was. I learned that the transmission doesn't like it when you try to shift without engaging the clutch. Needless to say I was thankful I lived out in the country. Somehow I think Papa thanked God we did too;
especially when he took me "driving".

I'm finding myself these days in neutral again.
    I've got new gears to learn.

Funny thing is I'm not sure what I'm driving.

Losing one's mate can thrust one in such a place as "neutral".

I choose to be in an idling position right now.
    I do know where I am to go...Fairhope, Alabama.
        What to do? I'm waiting in neutral for new lessons in gear positions, how to shift and when.

> I'm not worried or fretful...I am at peace
> I know who's "car" I'm in.

Just as Papa lovingly taught me to drive an old Buick...I feel safe in the Master's loving care.

The old song says it so well, "Many things about tomorrow
I don't seem to understand.
But I know who holds tomorrow
and I know who holds my hand."

Learning to drive had its traumas.

Learning to live again, without Bryant will also have its traumas.

One trauma is saying good-bye to a dear church family.
You have been nothing less than Christ to me and my family in these past four years, especially during our ordeal with cancer. We have had every need met through your sacrificial love. Bryant and I enjoyed sharing a ministry with you. We loved loving each and every one of you. We loved teaching you, learning with you, crying with you, marrying some of you and grieving with you over your disappointments and ours.

God knew what He was doing when He sent us to Normandale. He gave us the most wonderful church family a parsonage family could hope for. Your unconditional love and service to my family and the community show your great desire to be ambassadors for Christ. You, Normandale United Methodist Church have done an excellent job of being Christ to others.

For a season you are also, in Neutral. Idling, waiting for new leadership and new direction. You too, are learning to "drive" again.

My prayers for you are that God will bless you richly for all you have given to me and my family. I pray for a brighter day for you...and for me. I pray for your needs to be met through Christ. I pray that all who come behind you will find you have been faithful to the cause of Christ and His purposes.

Yes!!! This is painful!!!! This is so hard to do!!!! Nothing worth having is easy in life.

Jessica and I take with us fondest memories of you and your love. We leave behind a daughter, son-in-law and a precious grandson.

This hurts! Change usually is painful. I pray only good to come out of this for you and for us.

We are all in "Neutral". The winds of change are blowing.
I'm learning to "drive" again.
You will too.

May God envelope us, fill us, guide us as we get "the hang of it".

What is "it"?...............
Life without Bryant.

The Rev. C. Bryant Wilson and his wife, Pam, discuss the bone marrow transplant he received recently in Birmingham.

PATRICIA MIKLIK/STAFF

A TEST of FAITH

The Rev. C. Bryant Wilson battles a life-threatening illness with faith, the love of his family and the support of his congregation

By Nancy Fonti
ADVERTISER STAFF WRITER

The Rev. C. Bryant Wilson knows that sometimes even ministers need ministering.

In January 1995, doctors diagnosed the Rev. Mr. Wilson, 51, with lymphoma, cancer of the lymph glands.

The cancer began in the minister's large intestine and quickly spread to his stomach and small intestine.

After eight months of chemotherapy, his health had improved and he and his wife, Pam, "thought we had it licked." Two months later, the cancer returned.

His oncologist, Dr. Keith Thompson of the Montgomery Cancer Center, recommended that the Rev. Mr. Wilson get a bone marrow transplant, so he went to the University of Alabama at Birmingham Hospital on April 18 and stayed for six weeks.

The Rev. Mr. Wilson, pastor of Normandale United Methodist Church, and Mrs. Wilson, his wife of 22 years, aren't sure of his condition now.

Doctors say a person is cured if the disease does not recur in five years.

The Wilsons, who have three children and two grandchildren, say it's a matter of waiting it out.

But throughout the failed chemother-

WANT TO HELP?

What: Benefit dinner and golf tournament for the Rev. C. Bryant Wilson.
When: The dinner is 7 p.m. Friday. The golf tournament is 11 a.m. July 1.
Where: The dinner is at Normandale United Methodist Church, 706 E. Patton Ave. The golf tournament is at Linksman Golf Course in Mobile.
Cost: The dinner is $10 per person, and the golf tournament cost is $200 per team.
Other donations: Contributions to C. Bryant Wilson Fund can be made at any First Alabama Bank.
Information: Call Normandale United Methodist Church, 288-6340.

"This is a case where the congregation had to minister to their pastor and his family," the Rev. Mr. Wilson said. "The tables have turned, and they have been wonderful."

Hundreds of cards and notes filled the Wilsons' mailbox. The telephone rang with encouragement and wishes for a swift recovery.

congregation joined hands and prayed for a successful operation.

"God's presence in our lives doesn't really help us escape our problems," the Rev. Mr. Wilson said. "But throughout the problems, he is there."

The operation, which cost $250,000 was not covered by the Rev. Mr. Wilson's insurance. To help pay for the operation, church members are holding a benefit dinner at 7 p.m. Friday at Normandale United Methodist Church, 706 E. Patton Ave. Tickets are $10.

There also will be a benefit golf tournament July 1 at Linksman Golf Course in Mobile. Cost is $200 per team.

So far, the Rev. Mr. Wilson's congregation, other nearby churches of all denominations and other sources have raised about $35,000 for the minister and his family.

Throughout his battle with cancer, the Normandale pastor kept his congregation updated on his physical and emotional condition through reflective writings.

"These are letters people can identify with," Mrs. Wilson said. "This (cancer) is what we call a valley. A valley may not be cancer, but we all go through valleys."

Through his writing, the Rev. Mr. Wilson demonstrates what Dr. Thomp-

Story Corner

Thanksgiving is God's gift

Thanksgiving comes as a gift from God every day of our lives. Every day—regardless of the circumstances.

Our Wilson family, which celebrates the Thanksgiving national holiday each year with a family reunion in north Alabama, has already celebrated Thanksgiving this year. "We can do this any month of the year," said my husband in a memorial service on Oct. 30.

Our October 19 reunion was special. Thirty-nine of us gathered in Montgomery to give thanks with my brother, Bryant, pastor of Normandale United Methodist Church there. A few tears, as always, were shed even at the big party we threw at a cousin's home. But mostly, as always, we gathered around a big potluck, clustered here and there to rejoice in one another, threw footballs back and forth in the front yard and watched a little on TV, and welcomed three babies to their first family Thanksgiving.

The next day in worship Bryant told the congregation, "I think the family gathered for me." He had strength enough for a few opening remarks and to baptize two and receive six confirmands into membership before returning home.

On Monday he admitted painfully that he had probably preached his last sermon. But he had not. The next morning he sat at the computer and wrote his last church newsletter column, "But if not."

It was based on the story of Shadrach, Meshach, and Abednego in the Book of Daniel who declared their faith that God was able to deliver them from the fiery furnace. "But if not...we will not serve your gods," they said to King Nebuchadnezzar.

"Hang in there with me, Sis," he said to me the next day. "Our God is a healing God, and I'm holding out for a miracle." I hugged his skin-and-bones cancer-ridden body and praised God for a brother with a "but if not" faith, not a "fair weather" faith.

"Faith is not faith unless it has passed the test of not getting what it wants," he had written in his last column: "the unhealed body, the untimely death, the divorce that came anyway, the promised promotion that turned out to be an empty promise, the friend who misunderstood anyway. The list can go on and on...."

When Bryant's voice and spirit weakened, but never his mind and heart, his beloved wife Pam held him in her strong arms and reminded him: "You are going through a transition: you are exiting and you are entering. And it is our privilege and honor to be here, Bettie and I, to help you exit and to help you enter."

And then it was Sunday again. During that night we—his immediate family and the Hospice nurse—were there when he drew his last breath. It was a blessed and sacred moment in time.

On All Saints' Eve celebrative services in his memory were completed. He had shown through his dying how to live in the faith.

On this Thanksgiving Day our family will gather again in north Alabama from far and wide. For three days we'll eat, talk ourselves hoarse, hike in the mountains, fall in the lake (accidentally, of course), play volleyball and golf, worship in Holy Communion, and remember our October reunions and our communion with the saints who have gone before us. We'll shed some tears; it wouldn't be a Wilson reunion without them.

And we will sing hymns of joy to God for the blessings bestowed on us all, for the grace to be faithful in life and in death, and for the community of the church which has sustained us through another year.

Is not that your hymn of praise? In your family, your church, your community, and yes, in our ragged world on our daily Days of Thanksgiving?

In the words of Isaac Watts' hymn, "...when my voice is lost in death, Praise shall employ my nobler powers: My days of praise shall ne'er be past, While life, and thought, and being last, Or immortality endures."

That's a "but if not" faith that sings.

—Bettie Wilson Story

Sayings on prayer...

Prayer is not only the participation in communication with God in the encounter of religious experience, but it is also the "readying" of the spirit for such communication. It is the total process of quieting down and to that extent must not be separated from meditation.

—Howard Thurman
The Creative Encounter

Bettie Wilson Story (Bryant's sister)

ISBN-13: 978-0-9987724-5-5

ISBN-13: 978-0-9987724-5-5

ISBN-13: 978-0-9987724-5-5

ISBN-13: 978-0-9987724-5-5

ISBN-13: 978-0-9987724-5-5

ISBN-13: 978-0-9987724-5-5

www.ingramcontent.com/pod-product-compliance
Lightning Source LLC
Chambersburg PA
CBHW061456040426
42450CB00008B/1380